Paper Lanterns

Paper Lanterns

□

Poems by Gerry Sloan

Half Acre Press
Fayetteville
2011

ISBN-13: 978-0-9829455-6-8

Designed by Liz Lester

HALF
ACRE
PRESS
halfacrepress.com

To my mother, Lynndon Sloan, keeper of the flame

"Souls of the dead ride to heaven on the backs of turtles"
—Peace Park inscription for the
45,000 Koreans who also lost their lives

Each year, on August 6th, paper lanterns are placed before nightfall into the rivers of Hiroshima, inscribed with messages of bereavement and peace, in the hope for a future without nuclear weapons or war. Traditional Japanese belief states that humans came from water, so the lanterns represent bodies returning to the sea, illumination for the 140,000 spirits who died in 1945 as a result of the first atomic bomb.

Art can be lanterns, and people can be lanterns. The lanterns in my life have been teachers, students, family, friends. You know who you are. This book is dedicated to you, and to the light we must continue to shed and share. It is for Jun Okada, whose eleven-year-old father, knocked down by the blast on his way to school, continued to search for his lunchbox, and survived. It is for my eighteen-year-old father who surveyed the devastation and remained silent for forty years. It is for my Japanese "daughters" (exchange students) Tomoko Nitta, Makiko Kanaizumi, and Tomoko Akagi, that they may raise their children safely, without fear. It is for my neighbor, Hisae Kimura Yale, whose artwork graces the cover. It is for Dick Bennett, my compass in choppy waters. It is a quiet plea for dignity and sanity, as we drift intertwined down the river of time.

CONTENTS

III. Imagined Lives

IV. Missing Persons

V. Mums

VI. Lyrics Perhaps

ACKNOWLEDGMENTS

The author wishes to express his appreciation to the editors of the following anthologies or journals in which some of these poems previously appeared, often in slightly altered form:

Along the River: An Anthology of Contemporary Arkansas Poetry: "Rock-Skipping on the West Fork," "Octaves"

Alura Quarterly: "Rock-Skipping on the West Fork"

Annual Review of Jazz Studies: "Little Jazz Elegies"

Black Bear Review: "Fish-Kill on the White River"

The Christian Science Monitor: "The Visitor"

DEROS (Date of Estimated Return from Overseas): "Vietnam"

Gryphon: "Osage Orange"

The Lyric: "April Foal"

A Necessary Scavenger: "Silence," "American Trash," "Coronal"

Northwest Arkansas Times: "Leaving Heavener"

Old Hickory Review: "Rock-Skipping on the West Fork"

Plains Poetry Journal: "Octaves"

Poem: "Petoskey Stone from Rebecca"

Rainbows and Rhapsodies: "Confederate Cemetery in Winter"

Studia Mystica: "Field Days"

Thirteen: "Greenhouse Addendum"

The Truth of the Trees: "Kissing the Corpse," "Downwind from Dachau"

Viaztlan: "The Scar"

Voices International: "Black on White"

Writers Bloc 3: "Tightrope Walkers"

Quotes by E. Fay Jones are taken from "My Most Important Thoughts," from the Fay Jones Collection, Special Collections, University of Arkansas Libraries, and are used with permission.

I.

Leaving Heavener

Do not fail to write down your first impressions.
They will never come again, once they have faded.

—LYNNDON SLOAN, diary, January 1, 1999

Invocation

Blue moon (though really yellow),
the second in one May,
whether you bode well, O
this we cannot say.

Morning will consume
your field of indigo
where constellations bloom.
Eventually you'll show

your hand, flesh
out the dreams we brew.
Teach us to distinguish
the diamonds from the dew.

The Poet's Winter Night

The Arctic Express
has dumped another
load of snow
on Arkansas.

The jet stream slips
further south each year
like an old man's
baggy underwear.

Sitting alone
in a drafty room,
he sharpens his pencil
and waits

for a friendly nod
from the absentee Muse,
then gives up waiting
and writes.

The Visitor

A solitary sentinel appeared,
unannounced, on the coldest
night of the year's end—
a red-and-black ant
with the enlarged
head and jaw of a soldier—
upon the bear's-claw quilt
pieced together years ago
by someone's grandmother.
Looking up from my book
with faint astonishment, I am
drawn into this world of furtive
feet and feelers, whose mission
in such inclement weather
baffles my comprehension—
tracing their labored
progress across the
faded terrain of
parti-colored
patchwork.

Silence

"There is no such thing."

—JOHN CAGE

Philosophers and scientists remind us
it's only a working hypothesis.
Mornings like this, I'm inclined to agree,
our Potscrubber 900 grinding gaily
in the background, the sound of traffic
rising from the street. Schopenhauer
was maddened to distraction by the crack
of coachwhips. In our time we long for their
quaint charm. Even in a soundproof room,
we can't escape the music of our bodies.
Faint anthems of the central nervous system,
ground bass of the blood, soon mobilize
against the silence blooming on a page,
filling the vacuum beyond its edge.

Sand Crabs

i.

In Oceanview in '52
they might have been hatched
by an overactive imagination.
Back in Oklahoma, nothing
moved so fast. Crab-pots dangled
from barnacled piers. Spent
bivalve shells in the tide-pool
often sported drilled
holes of the moonsnail
on its predatory rounds.
Battleships cruising the Chesapeake
whispered rumors of faraway wars,
my father one man in a uniform.

ii.

Half a century later, the wars
have migrated elsewhere.
The Bay's life-forms
are threatened, or gone,
the old sailors dead
or in nursing homes.
From the landlocked
shores of middle age,
I can conjure the scent
of sea-salt still, wet sand
squishing between bare toes,
pale apparitions darting
just the beyond my field of vision.

Leaving Heavener

Sometimes I can close my eyes
and see the hills and buildings of childhood
transposed impossibly backward,
magically preserved from the ravages of time,
the long-dead resurrected: Layton and Rose
on the screened-in backporch
for some after-dinner dominoes,
a whippoorwill keening the distance.

Gone these twenty-some-odd years,
my grandmother looks down at me
from her picture on the hutch,
taken in her teens before
the kids and a bad marriage.
Who knows what became of
that kitten, that hat, those houses
sagging in the background?
Who knows if the violets
bloom on her grave,
or whether the dead
also grieve?

3925 South Broadway

You remember the addresses of houses
which no longer exist, confirmed
in photographs, the deceased occupants
still smiling at vanished flowerbeds,

proud of their lost labors. Thirty years,
forty years or more have come and gone,
erasing entire neighborhoods. You
pause, pluck a reddish hollyhock

to press into a book. Your mother may
have planted this or its progenitor.
You pick up a fragment of red brick
from the back alley, place into your purse

to function like a keepsake, something
you might take out later on when far away
to remind you of brick buildings packed
endlessly together, a woman

hunched over her ironing, sweat
beading her upper lip, her body odor
something you can't entirely forget.
Frieda is dead, and Drizzle Drawers, hysterical

immigrants who thought cleanliness was God.
Vernon's Liquor Store is now a vacant lot.
The carnival supply has moved next door
into a more modern facility,

leaving the old lettering to fade.
Nearby the Mississippi labors bravely
in its traces, bound downstream like memory
bearing its toxic burden to the Gulf.

American Trash

"No deposit. No return."

When I was small
a man would haul
our trash off
in a mule-drawn cart—
a necessary scavenger.
He had a dozen
barefoot kids
who never had
enough to eat,
the butt of many
local jokes.

"We'll send you to live with Ed Hall,"
our irate moms admonished.
We'd pass their place at night
on our way to shoot rats
at the city dump—fat
mutants we would indispose
with flashlights and a .22
(they'd leap three feet straight up).
That was back before garbage
became an institution,
inundating half the globe.

Friend, if I could say this
more cleverly, more
artfully—you can rest
assured I would.
But cleverness has been

our bane, and we're beyond
the help of art. I haven't seen
a rat in years, and Ed Hall's
white trash kids
have grown and prospered,
respectable as you or I
who leave our weekly refuse
on the curbsides of suburbia,
still not quite convinced
it disappears.

Big Bang

"a random fluctuation of energy"

—Art Hobson

Some girls went down to the depot
to watch the troop train arrive,
to wave at all the young soldiers.

An older soldier wrote his name
and address on a slip of paper
then dropped it out of the window,

retrieved by a teenager with gray eyes
and auburn hair. She wrote to him.
He wrote to her. They corresponded

then got married after the war,
to her parents' disapproval.
She gave him four sons. Then

died in childbirth. The soldier
drank himself numb. Then remarried.
His sons grew up. Became soldiers.

Found other bored girls to marry.
Survived another war. Then another.
Died variously of heart attacks,

lung cancer, Parkinson's.
Each accompanied by a death
certificate. A slip of paper.

Which is where it all began.
Felled trees. Dark energy.
Dark matter.

—— II. ——

Field Days

"Echoing Webster's definition of symbiosis as the intimate living together of two dissimilar organisms in a mutually beneficial relationship, he suggests that the life-giving, life-enhancing reality lies neither in the house nor in the hill, but in the place between. It is in the realm of interaction and interchange (in responses) where the magical and metaphorical leap can be made and a passing can occur from one cosmic zone to another."

—E. Fay Jones

Osage Orange

Autumn inflates the horse-apples
in trees behind the house
like leaden green balloons.
Neither orange nor Indian
they litter the lawn at mowing time,
the only certain harvest here
where formerly was pasture grass.
Stacking them to clear a path—
our bumper crop of useless fruit—
we wonder what to do with them.
Stash them on a pantry shelf
for roach-bane, if we choose?
Or see to it the neighbor kids
don't toss them at passing cars?

Weeks later we look out to see
the yellow leaves, the scenery.
Having outlived their usefulness
as fence-posts, hedges, longbows,
the trees retaliate by leaving
sticky cairns of cannonballs
beside the chain-link fence.
Winter will advance and freeze
them in a blackened pulpy mess—
a trove of seeds where hungry birds
will redefine their usefulness.

Black on White

The crow in the snow
is a connoisseur
of scraps
circumscribes our heap
with his elegant steps
careful
not to get feet
in the gravy

He sorts out
potato peelings
grapefruit rinds
till at last he finds
a heel of bread

Rising to a fencepost
to signal his confreres
he ruffles black feathers
then throws back his head
to release the raucous
cry of his being
which reverberates
over the frozen pond
into the snowy hills beyond

The Star That Got Its Wish

(for Brady)

The season's first wet snow produces
snowmen by the hundreds, whole
families in many yards,
going about their business
with carrot noses, pebble
eyes, mimicking us
passers-by
with token caps
and scarves. It's hard to tell
if they are waving hello
or goodbye. Tonight
the clouds will
disappear. The crescent moon and Pleiades
will glisten their approval, knowing
tomorrow a brighter star
must pass by here,
calling its crystalline
children home.

Backroads to Eureka

(for Lyndall)

These roads have grown familiar
as the need to see my daughter,
grown herself and living
in a town not far away.

Days like this the earth seems bent
beneath its vernal burden,
heavy with the green they say
distinguishes us from the moon and nearer planets.

In a matter of weeks the spring roadkill
will dissolve beyond recognition,
collapse into heaps of cartilage
and furry vertebrae.

How then to identify
these figures masquerading
as raccoon, armadillo, deer,
withdrawn into their archetypes?

And what of man, that creature
caught in mortality's highbeam?
Shall we say he was deficient
in magnanimity? Shall we say

his passing altered all?
The green keeps on repeating
in endless duplication, the fauna
charging into cars

as if we might illuminate
the vastnesses between the stars,
or this darker space within a father's
all-too-human heart.

Cry of the Turtle

(for Allison)

When my daughter witnessed a box turtle
crushed by two rednecks in a blue pickup,
nothing would do but to bundle it up
in a vain attempt at rescue, though I soon

pronounced the wound fatal. "Ease the creature
into a ditch and mutter a hasty Hail Mary,"
I advised. But she insisted, the Mother
Teresa of Roadkill. She later swore

it wept real tears in the agony of passing.
Next day we buried it in the backyard
between her pet duck and a rabbit. I tried
to explain how rednecks hunt quail, how

turtles are said to be raiders of nests,
but she wouldn't hear of it. Sometimes
just drawing a breath is a terrorist act.
Sometimes we'd like to flee our own species.

But I take pride in my daughter's doomed
gesture, honor our brief presence here,
whether or not turtles actually cry,
whether or not anyone listens.

Sixth Grade Science Notes of My Son
Who Has a Hearing Loss

Sounds are vibrations. Vibrations are made
when an object moves back and forth.

Sounds can make you feel peaceful,
happy, nervous, unhappy, or alert.

Some sounds serve as warnings.
Some can be harmful.

Very loud sounds
can damage the human ear.

Objects that are vibrating
cause the air around them

to vibrate too. These vibrations
produce sound waves. Hard

surfaces reflect sound waves
(echo is an example).

Soft surfaces absorb them
(carpet is an example).

Sound travels through air
and other gases. It can also

travel through liquids and solids.
Sound cannot travel through empty space.

See the page on Ear.

Herring Loss

America's disaffected sons
dream of reconciliation
with their fathers.
If it happens at all, it happens
too late, lacking resolution.

The state record skipjack herring
weighs in at just two pounds,
the long-ear perch eight ounces—
a fourth the size of skipjack
but big enough to tip the scale
and end up on this calendar
by the Game and Fish Commission.

We dream of going fishing
with our disaffected fathers,
becoming friends as well as sons,
drifting through long afternoons
with nothing special on our minds
but casting. This isn't how
it happens.

Turn up your hearing-aid. Cut
bait. A record alligator gar
will glide past on the last day
of the year, weigh in at 215,
inhale the record herring
like an after-dinner snack,
glide on and never once
look back.

Father, shall we gather
at the river? Father, lift your ear
out of the water.

Petoskey Stone from Rebecca

Sculpted by the wind's rough hand,
the raspy cat's-tongue of the rain,
it makes a proper present
from one maker to another.
I see you wading, shoes in hand,
girlish, on the shores of Crete—
but this is just an image triggered
by your recent trip, a pebble
cast into the mind's still pool.

Patterned, with an olive tinge,
it almost seems a poem itself,
more-or-less anonymous
(you'll know what I mean by this),
fashioned from past coral generations.
Improbable that it should stray
so far from your native Michigan,
a journey unremarkable
by meteoric standards.

No thunderstone this, simply
one small mute reminder how
time has its way with matter.
Drawn in to such an orbit,
it settles into sedentary
shelf-life on my windowsill,
an idle curiosity,
a gift in its uniqueness at last
equal to the giver.

Layers

"The houses are all gone under the sea.
The dancers are all gone under the hill."

—T.S. Eliot

Before, this suburban subdivision
was a strawberry patch (I remember
it well), and before that was a woodland
meadow (before my time), and before that
a small forest cleared by weary settlers
marking their trek through the wilderness,
and judging from the fossils in protruding
limestone knees, it was once a shallow sea
where mud-sharks ruled the food-chain,
                              and before
that was something molten, without form,
inconceivable to those who scribble
sonnets without rhyme, those who slam
their doors and then depart for work in cars,
peeling back the layers and layers of darkness.

Field Days

I pass the ginko daily
on my way uphill to work,
resist the knee-jerk tendency
to lapse into metaphor:
to see it as a slender girl,
Oriental possibly, posing
in her leafy shift
of late-October gold;
shocked another day to find her
naked in a fairy ring,
stripped the night before
by wind and rain.

Perhaps I'm seen myself to be
a sort of mobile tree,
like the blindman healed in Luke.
Metaphors work either way.
This one's said to be
a living fossil;
to which I can relate.
I cast a backward glance to where
it anchors the horizon.

Unframed by the human eye,
it stands there like an orphaned
silhouette against the sky,
spreading tiny rumors
of survival.

Study in Contrast

From the confines of retirement,
my father speculates why birds
shit white on his black fence and shit
black on his white house, as if some
malign intelligence were at work,
some plot to darken his
otherwise tranquil existence.

I, who have squandered my life
in academia, am told by my daughter,
who spent hers in the service sector,
that I am supremely unqualified to ponder
so profound an ontological matter, having never
sweetened a tip by soothing a surly customer
while balancing a loaded tray on one
hip, shuffling off instead each day
to the ivory tower of art.

But I am no stranger to the shadow-play
of nature, having observed the birds
of worry and care from an altogether
different perspective, noting how
black and white seem to recombine
in unforeseen collusion, how shit,
whether real or virtual, seems
always to run downhill.

As You Were

We'd all be unaffected
as the Confederate officer
said to have given the order:
"Prepare to git on your horses,
GIT"—which made up in directness
for what it lacked in decorum;
or Ray Charles singing "chimbley tops"
in "Somewhere Over the Rainbow,"
knowing the homefolks would cringe
if he pronounced it right.
Dante in the vernacular
soared over the empyrean,
but Latin would have gotten him
nowhere. Burns in the King's
English would be forgotten.

We'd like to be sincere
without becoming maudlin.
We'd like to tell the truth,
with beauty for a handmaid.
Fond wish, for it more often
sinks to rhetoric. We're left
with just a story.

A man once taught a boy
how to cup his hands
for calling doves: a rising cry
followed by three deeper ones.
They practiced it in secret

then waited in the bois d'arc grove,
struck by how easily birds
are duped by some familiar tune,
or desperate as we for what
seems like communication.

III.

Imagined Lives

"Old men should be explorers?"
I'll be an Indian.
Iroquois.

—THEODORE ROETHKE,
"The Longing" from *The Far Field*

Nature Channel

You hesitate above the cluttered TV tray.
The coyotes have come once more for the baby elk.

The mother stands her ground for as long as possible,
pausing between rounds to lick the baby's face.

She knows, deep down, this signifies goodbye.
There are five of them and only one of her.

Patiently they circle the doomed pair
in this ancient game whose rules are foreknown.

And time, like some wind-up automaton, some
merciless predictible rerun, seems always on their side.

The Last Wild Turkey in Manhattan

She only made it to the 28th floor
of an Upper West Side high-rise,
perched sedately on the balcony
like a tourist taking a breather;

or worse, like some avian Ishi
who strayed into civilization
in a final act of desperation,
disoriented or simply curious.

Wild turkeys can fly vertically
only a dozen feet or so. How she
rose so high and why is anyone's guess,
intent on scaling some "turkey Everest."

The *Times* can only report the fact,
plus a photo by the startled occupant
who is rethinking his theory of omens.
Charles Fort would have loved this, this

crazed creature gone balcony-hopping
in the unlikliest of settings, pausing
briefly to catch her breath, ungainly bird
who forces us to ponder the absurd.

Tightrope Walkers

At daybreak
walkers and joggers
dot the sidewalks
of suburbia

as overhead
a fox squirrel
walks its tightrope
highline wire

furball Wallenda
itself a live wire
choosing each step
with jerky care

past master of
the kind of balance
which eludes us
here below

Lost and Found

You learn to look for beauty
in the commonplace: a starling
on the parking lot, foraging
for God-knows-what, its
blue-notes echoing between
the ugliest of buildings;
dry leaves caught in crevices,
remembering their furlough
from the trees; prismatic
petrol-blooms on wet asphalt,
rainbows that leave
no trace of gold.

Yesterday they found the body
of a missing teenage girl,
the victim of a homicide.
You imagine the parents' anguish
over all they did or failed
to do, the mingled sense
of relief and loss.
A truck groans in the distance.
The starling seizes its trophy.
You wonder if the search for beauty
balances a day like this.
You wonder if our seeking
will redeem us.

Off the Grid

he wants to get
completely off the grid

drop more-or-less
permanently out-of-sight

become like Ambrose Bierce
a missing person

disassemble
take flight

seek refuge beyond
the LAST EXIT sign

. . . .

wake up one fine day
in a rattletrap truck
full of sub-Saharan nomads

who keep stopping to hammer
under the hood
with assorted broken wrenches

then have to push
to get started again
because of a broken starter

five miles later
in the middle of nowhere
repeating the same damn ritual

stopping the truck
getting out to resume
their obligatory banging

. . . .

which feels like it's coming
from inside of his head

the canteen meanwhile
running frightfully low

as he stares into a baby's face
slung over a dusty shoulder

a face that hasn't
moved for days

as flies keep crossing
and crossing the matted eyes

Stoplight

In the car ahead of me
a woman is beating her baby,
routinely, without passion,
striking it repeatedly then
slamming it into a car-seat,
scolding unintelligibly.
Across from her the driver,
a boyfriend or husband, sits
stoic as a boulder, eyes
forward, feigning unconcern.
Maybe this happens so often
he truly doesn't notice.
Maybe he's upset with her.
Or maybe she's upset with him
and hits the child instead.
I have no way of knowing,
their drama played out silently
between two sets of windshields,
my speculation useless as the woman's
futile gesture, buying time in idled
traffic, backed up as far as we
can see, waiting
for the light to change.

M(issing) I(n) A(ction)

Forget the dental records, lab results.
When the old man with his arthritic hand
balanced the egg on a chopstick stuck
in a duplicate weathered unmarked grave
(the spot a paid psychic led them to),
he knew at once it was his soldier son
vanished thirty-some-odd years before,
late since then for every single meal,
a gaping hole ripped out of their lives.
Tonight the old man would return, sleep
peacefully for the first time in decades,
rediscover at last the lost gift of rest,
knowing that which could now be removed,
knowing that the hen's egg never wavered.

Another Poem for James Wright

One day I dallied
to pat the black horse
in a pasture white with snow.

Head extended through the fence,
he arched his neck so gracefully
it made me think of you,

moldering in Ohio, and I reached
out to stroke his rough ear,
to whisper a reminder

that the grass isn't always
greener here
in the land of the yet living.

Elizabeth Bishop on the Poetry Circuit

The damask drapes droop sadly
in this ill-appointed room
where setting sunlight slants
across the dingy beige pile carpet.

Damask rose. Damascus steel.
Oldest road in Syria.
Here instead a herd of Herefords
munching cud at sunset. How thoroughly

remarkable. Adjust your trusty
binoculars with the customary care.
Observe their masticating jaws
deliciously out-of-sync,

how white and brown mesh
on those massive shoulders.
Tomorrow, in another town,
speak to respectful students

on the felicities of art, lines
broken with discretion, choices
informed by observation and good
taste (antithesis of chain motels

and faceless restaurants). Red
Lobster. Ramada Inn. Ramadan,
month of fasting. Does denial
ever guarantee redemption?

Focus instead on the cattle,
all facing the same direction,
tails bent toward the fence.
Notice how sunlight gradually

recedes across the pasture.
Ponder awhile Wilde's saucy quip:
anything worth knowing
can't be taught.

IV.

Missing Persons

Woman's voice:

"I've always wept over Hiroshima's fate. Always."

Man's voice:

"No. What was there for you to weep over?"

—*Hiroshima mon amour*

I am the enemy you killed, my friend.

—Wilfred Owen, "Strange Meeting"

Dirigible

"Oh, the humanity . . ."

—HERB MORRISON, reporting the
destruction of the Hindenburg, 1937

Angling for bream on Lake Elmdale,
our peace is shattered momentarily
by a passing Remax hot-air balloon
huffing like a rainbow dragon.

We continue watching our bobbers,
our minds soaring high overhead
in that region where humanity
appears like a legion of ants,

thinking how the man at Harvard said
if ants were suddenly to become extinct,
over two hundred species would perish
as a consequence, whereas if mankind

were to disappear, many species, if not
the entire planet, would more than likely
flourish; thinking how we continue to kill
each other, to rape, plunder, pillage, burn;

thinking how the warfare between termites
and ants is the oldest conflict on earth;
thinking how in Aboriginal lore, humans
are just a dream in the minds of termites,

how in the rain forest of Brazil, we're viewed
ourselves as the termites, insatiable for wood;
thinking of Icarus who soared close to the sun
then plunged back in a conflagration we're still

trying to fathom, mimicry the highest praise,
our fiery airy acrobats leaping onto the runway,
inspiring others to find their wings and follow them,
burning, burning, burning like the Buddha's holy vision.

Paper Lanterns

(August 6, 1985)

A teenage sailor on shore leave,
my father walked the streets of Hiroshima
shortly after the bomb, but waited
nearly forty years to tell us
what he'd seen—which was apparently
nothing. Nothing, nothing, nothing.

Hearing Mahler's Fifth today on public radio,
I wonder how such stark extremes
can occupy a given century—such
peaks and troughs of human experience.
I have friends who assure me nuclear energy
is larger than lyric poetry, and

judging from the anthologies, I must
hasten to agree. But on this inauspicious day,
I think of my father hustling merchandise
fifty miles away, of paper lanterns floating
on the Ohta, and plug my ears to their advice
and have my little say.

The Scar

Sitting beside a June campfire
counting the stars and whippoorwills,
I leaned upon a heated stone
and bellowed
like a yearling steer
at branding time. Complications
set in and days later
my forearm was swollen double.

Ice packs calmed the cauterized
flesh. And time attended
to the rest, leaving only this
Rorschach blot. Sometimes it looks
like a turkey—one of those
silhouettes you see in schools
at Thanksgiving. At other times,
a weathercock combing the wind.

Finally someone suggested
a mushroom, and everything
fell into place.
The mark of Cain
has migrated to my left
arm, where it blossoms
like a flower imprint
on Hiroshima cement.

Fish-Kill on the White River

These corpses aren't symbolic. Symbols
can kill but aren't corruptible as these
crappie, shad and bluegills, these
smallmouth bass, their upturned bellies
white and putrefying in the sun.

It doesn't take long—a matter
of minutes—their element
deprived of oxygen,
in this case a surfeit
of grease: effluent
from the Campbell Soup plant
miles upstream, brought down
by heavy rains.
     Now the clouds
disperse, the Campbell Kids
cavorting on the bank like cherubim
or refugees from ad-men's brains.
In another dimension, they
market bison stew
to starving Indians,
their profit margin wide
as clear-cut forestland.

Behold these unsymbolic dead,
undone by urban sprites—plump
children innocent as we
who commandeer the ecospace,
our euphemized technology
insidious as chicken grease.

Greenhouse Addendum

Leafbuds on the mulberry tree
are confused by the April snow,
not knowing whether to
come out and freeze, or hold back
a few more days. Fingertips bursting
with chlorophyll, they reach out to read
the wind's icy braille
and the intent of a sky
whose mood has grown glacial.
Air currents once predictable
roam the globe like riderless
horses. The car keys
jingle in my pocket
like coffin nails.

Vietnam

(for Skip Hays)

"Vietnam, we've all been there."
—MICHAEL HERR *(Dispatches)*

It would seem, in our time,
that conscience became

vestigial, like wisdom
teeth or tail bones,

an appendix to help us
digest the raw meat

required by
the national appetite.

We managed to stay
two steps ahead

of the yawning norns
of the local board

but finally gave in,
through various means,

I to teach and you
to write. Years later,

our regret is not
for buddies lost,

or experience missed,
but for backward boys

who were sent
in our place

because of their I.Q.,
or income, or race.

Downwind from Dachau

This April day they slash and burn to make
way for another housing development,
balancing their ledgers
of profit and loss
against legions of the rootless.

This far away in space and time, we can
almost imagine they never occurred,
those other days up-ended,
the blown ash
delicately dusting our bare skin.

For Elie Weisel

When the G.I.s
liberated Auschwitz,
they wept at first
then cursed

what they found,
cursed Man, cursed
God, cursed all
of His creation.

On the ears of one
emaciated boy,
their curses fell
like prayers,

prayers left
still unanswered
after nearly
fifty years.

He takes in hand
a pencil, then
commits this heresy
on clean white paper.

fodder

in the aftermath of gettysburg
hogs gourmandized the corpses
left unburied overnight

in the muddy trenches at verdun
rats nibbled the lips and noses
off the blackened faces of the dead

after the typhoon at okinawa
sharks feasted on midshipmen
lashed securely to their rafts

what sacrifice oh heroes
fodder for sharks for rats for swine
where are all of you today

scattered by the winds of time

War in the Gulf

(footage on CNN)

i.

Soaked cormorants labor ashore.
Not "labor" in the human sense
producing bread or babies,
but something more austere.
It's only a matter of hours now,
their feathers mired in light
sweet crude, their fierce green
eyes fixed on the cameras—
a hard battle already lost
that could have been prevented.

ii.

Inebriates of light sweet crude,
    they stumble on the shore,
who must have misinterpreted
    the articles of war.
Do we see in their cancelled flight,
    these shorebirds of Kuwait,
a preview of our specie's plight,
    our all-too-human fate?

Missing Persons

Body parts keep falling from the sky.
We gather them in plastic bags
to reassemble later, simulacra
suddenly reduced to dental records,
moles, tattoos, plastic faces, DNA.

Sometimes the disappeared go
all-at-once, sometimes one by one.
Sometimes we orchestrate our grief;
sometimes we look the other way.
Missing persons line the street

in photocopied snapshots,
statistics once thought vital.
This one had small hands and tiny
fingers, this one a gap-toothed grin;
this one was four months pregnant.

ii.

Body parts keep falling from the sky.
We gather them in plastic bags
to reassemble later
on the television screen,
the weekly marathon of tits-and-ass,

the flicker-show of commerce, stage
on which the dead shall walk again,

body parts miraculously intact.
Call us if you see this person,
recognize through any means.

Help us determine who they were.
Help us determine where we are,
what solar system, galaxy, what
interstellar halfway house
among the stranded planets.

Windows

(for Kabin)

Rear windows. Bay windows. Windows
of opportunity, always opening for others.
Mis-timed, they often catch your hand,
outstretched at the moment of closing.

So you stand and stare at fortune's next fool,
convinced it should have been you in there,
brilliant in the flash-bulbs' blinding glare,
surrounded by thronging admirers.

Kissing the Corpse

Our native hardwoods are disappearing
faster than we can commemorate them
with subdivision names like Golden Oaks,
pulped to make pressed board for building houses
that won't last. Say they use formaldehyde.
Say they use ten thousand chemicals
we can't identify, surprised our corpses
will not rot. Looking out across
the Bradford pears and parking lot,
I wonder what will become of us, stuck
here at the wrong end of a century
gone bad. Late relatives arrive.
We gather to view the body, slip
in for one last kiss of the rigid lips.

Little Jazz Elegies

i. Hottentot Venus

You can call it irony,
life imitating something
or other, the Victorian era
lifting her ruffled skirts.

We market your imagery
then pocket the royalties.
Nothing much has changed;
it's just been rearranged.

The silicone clones of Hollywood
now flood the tanning salons
to mimic your dusky beauty,
inject their paltry appendages

to more closely resemble your own,
ghastly protrusions our grandmothers
would have giggled to ridicule,
content to be smugly superior.

We dragged you out of a cage
and onto a floodlit stage
and in the blinding flicker
christened you Josephine Baker.

ii. Blues for Jack Teagarden
(listening to "St. James Infirmary")

The morning sun reflects a bluish hood
on a starling going through its paces
in the yard, a clear sky overhead
as I start another record. Time passes
over moments like these—Town Hall '47,
the year that I was born—leaving tracks
retraceable in vinyl, the grooves uneven
as lives. The slide-and-waterglass were tricks
you learned in Texas, to coax a haunting chorus
from your horn.
      One January night I stood
outside to see Orion, his hunting chorus
lost among the cars, but found instead
another Rorschach figure on the stairs:
I saw a blues trombone player in the stars.

iii. In Memoriam: Alfonso Trent

The wading pool at Creekmore Park
is slowly filling up with leaves
like an empty robin's nest
    abandoned out of season.

Children of the middle class
are monkeys now instead of fish,
climbing up the rungs and bars
    provided by the city.

Decked out in their jogging suits
they test the outdoor bric-a-brac,
appearing to have lost the knack
    of knowing how to swim;

everything is structured here.
A Negro boy races down
the covered slide to happiness:
    Life is but a dream

he sings, his song no longer out
of bounds. Artillery from the Great
War, muzzle stuffed with sand, commands
    a busy tennis court

as if it still were no-man's-land.
Still I see the photograph
of your legendary band,
    captured by the shutter

in the attitudes of fashion,
sporting coats of camel's-hair
like ebony aristocrats
    unremembered now

in the city of your birth.
The trees dispatch another batch
of leaves, which rustle past our feet
    like anonymity.

iv. Second Line
(for my jazz history class)

Most people tiptoe through life
so as to arrive at death safely,
do arabesques on eggshells.

For them, Death has reserved
a special place of honor,
immaculately cushioned.

Others step to a rougher beat,
stomp off down cobbled streets
toward the wrong end of the Quarter,

rambling behind the band. No one
will reserve a place for them
or eulogize their slaughter.

It's like the cartoon short,
Bambi versus Godzilla, this
lopsided match between Love

and Death. Stomp off anyhow.
Learn to take time personally.
Mess around with the beat.

Start your inebriated chant:
Feet, don't fail me now,
feet, don't fail me yet.

Testing

This is a test.
This is only
a test.

At the sound of
the signal,
you would have been

informed what to do
in the event of an actual
emergency—how to lead

your loved ones through
the Valley of the Shadow,
the species like

a cancelled check.
It is essential to follow
instructions. It is

essential not to panic
or be guided by those
who haven't your own

best interest at heart.
You have spent your life
preparing for this—

an examination, of sorts.
But don't despair. Everyone
will pass. The curve will slide

clear off the scale, all
falling through eternity,
ecstatic with our blanket A.

Confederate Cemetery in Winter

Above our heads the leafless trees
are nameless as these headstones
ranging row on tidy row.
For such a war the Unknown Soldier
lay down in league and slept,
undisturbed by patient moles
passing overhead. Who would think

of breaking rank? After the fighting
at Pea Ridge, remnants of their gaunt
brigades tramped through town for days,
their dead discarded randomly. Descendants
came and segregated them by state,
restoring order of a kind, *Pro
Patria,* in stone and bronze.

The statue on its pedestal
looks away from Willow Heights,
low income housing for blacks,
as if it did not share our brief
concern for sleet or freezing rain—
as if content forever to have
lost a cause, a life, a name.

V.

MUMS

THINGS THAT ARE NEAR THOUGH DISTANT

Paradise.
The course of a boat.
Relations between a man and a woman.

> — *The Pillow Book of Sei Shōnagon,*
> translated by Ivan Morris

Mon Automne éternelle ô ma saison mentale

> —GUILLAUME APOLLINAIRE,
> "Signe" from *Alcools*

Aubade

At dawn, I reach to touch
the texture of your skin,
the velvet neck and thighs
grown too familiar now

yet still my chief delight.
You've earned your stripes
of stretch-marks, scars and
crow's-feet, streaking hair—

in which I played
no minor part. Our words
have changed and yet are still
the same as when we met,

attendants of the Lord
of Light. Would we,
if we could, unwish
this slow betrayal of the flesh?

Iris

n. 3. Gk. Myth. a messenger of the gods, regarded as the goddess
of the rainbow. 4. a rainbow. 5. any appearance resembling a rainbow.

—The American College Dictionary

It isn't O'Keefe's iris, burned
onto the canvas of memory;
or the girl at school whose mother
thought to name her for a flower;

but simply a blossom (some say "flag")
knocked off today while mowing,
placed into a bowl half-filled
with water. Set out by a woman

who grew too busy raising kids,
it still unfurls its standard
to the great lost cause of spring,

reminding us that passion is perennial
yet fragile as these flowers
named for rainbows.

Driving Through Fidelity

Returning to my wife
after a night in Kansas City,
I can't help but smile
driving through Fidelity,

a small town north of Diamond
just off I-44. A glance
reveals a peeled signboard—
Fidelity Insurance—

promising a coverage
far too good to be true.
I pass long rows of irises,
reminded of a woman who

herself is like a flower—
the subtle fragrance, seasonal
attraction. It's not exactly
loneliness I feel

when we're apart, but more
a kind of longing, as if something
were missing—a bee without pollen,
a lark without a wing.

Somewhere between the birthplaces
of George Washington Carver
and Harry Truman, men
faithful after their

fashion to the Peanut
and the Atom Bomb,
I think about the crazy
creatures we've become—

our constant contradictions,
predilection for metaphor—
towns named after conditions
for the lives we share and are.

This late in May, a road
could lead most anyplace,
hapless as magnetic tape
unspooling in the darkness;

instead it draws me closer
like a distant melody
lisped across the decades
sotto voce.

Dark Matter

The stars are out walking on stilts of light
    like clowns in a cosmic sideshow.
The sawdust below is dark energy, they say,
    pulling us irretrievably apart.

Set against this backdrop of darkness and departure,
    our gestures seem more fragile,
the occasional furtive touch or kiss
    to signify our progress.

You keep pressing me why I found you so late,
    but I came as soon as you called.
Will there be enough time to catch up with the light,
    for the clowns to step over our faces?

Burning Man

Medieval clerics tried to quell
adultery with a tether,
binding couples one year together
before whisking them off to Hell.
How much heat does it take to make
diamonds instead of charred carbon?
How many effigies to fear, one
by one, did we march to the stake?

You've had your whole life to prepare
for pop quizzes you keep failing,
as if the act of telling
might make anything more clear,
as if your actions were not meant
to fuel someone's resentment.

Midnight Croquet

You play it with the lights off.
No cheating in a game like this.
You play it out of habit
or an urgency that borders

on obsession. Pick a color
(as if it matters). Choose
your angles carefully, hoping
for a glint of moonlight

upon the dewy carpet. Don't
mistake your partner's ball
for that of an opponent.
A wooden click may signal

interference or else closure,
the peg on which to hang your
heart when all of this is over.
Eventually we'll all pass through

the wicket of the Milky Way
and none of this will matter—this
game in which we take such careful
aim, and miss. This marriage.

Whistle Tones

Drifting across the courtyard,
   these ghosts of tones
      which thrive above
         or instead of the ones

we aim for, hissing
   as from distant kettles
      left too long to boil,
         inhabiting a universe

adjacent to our own—
   one in which she isn't
      married to a dolt,
         and I am not

a bamboo flute
   abandoned by the window,
      tortured by the fingers
         of the wind.

Foliage

If trees were trust and leaves the slow betrayal
of days and light and chlorophyll,
would we choose a gaunt gray trunk
over festive autumn pennants drunk
on color? No contest, really,
between fickle or fidelity,
intoxicating elation
over bored preoccupation.

But when nature's party glitter
is reduced to fencerow litter,
we contemplate the evergreens,
what their contentment means
in terms so undeciduous,
the dawning realization: trees are us.

The Poem Lets Go of Its Pain

This is a poem about pain.
About pain that often masquerades
as pleasure, till you sense who's moving
behind the mask, that they have indeed
become the mask, one and inseparable.
You'd like to rip off the tawdry façade
but realize that is impossible,
that mask and face are one.

This is a poem about discovering
that someone you love is insane.
About the moment when you can no longer
deny the obvious. Or about the steady
accumulation of such moments, grim
and implacable. No longer deny
the false memories, the frequent
bizarre reversals, substituting

hate for love, goodbye for hello,
pretending it's all in the name
of some greater cause, some
reason larger than ourselves.
You see eyes blink behind the mask,
hear words formulating on the tongue,
words sure to be misunderstood,
stamped "please return to sender."

This poem is about growing pains
and the advancement of awareness.
About the shoot bidding farewell

to the seed, the seed to the root
reaching deeper into rich soil,
the adult plant lifting green
arms to the sun in an attitude
of renewal. A poem about that

most of all.

La Perfecta

"A fellow will remember a lot of things you wouldn't think he'd remember. You take me. One day, back in 1896, I was crossing over to Jersey on the ferry, and as we pulled out, there was another ferry pulling in, and on it there was a girl waiting to get off. A white dress she had on. She was carrying a white parasol. I only saw her for one second. She didn't see me at all, but I'll bet a month hasn't gone by since, that I haven't thought of that girl."

—Everett Sloane (Mr. Bernstein)
in *Citizen Kane*

Some things you will never know
and possibly were not meant to.
So you sublimate them into song,
keep confronting the Great Unknown.

It could be Bernstein's woman in white
emerging from *Citizen Kane,* glimpsed
once on the Jersey ferry, a sight
that would haunt him forever.

Or that day in the summer of '83,
the woman who stepped in
out of the rain
to shop at Kroch and Brentano's.

Or the hauntingly beautiful British girl
who smiled at you across the aisle,
might even have followed you
onto the train.

These are the visions of loveliness
that will ferry us to our graves,
with nary a trace of speech or touch
to mar their total perfection.

—for Pavel

Spherical Music

Our voices reach out across the space that intervenes,
    the necessary interval between us,
caress the vast recesses of the known universe
    somewhere in the vicinity of Venus

and beyond. Whose melodies that seek to unsettle
    the guarded heart, slip the soft traces of
the inner ear? Whose harmonies disrupt our consciousness
    with memories of long-forgotten love,

too painful to recall yet too beautiful to regret,
    such sweet-and-sour confusion of mind's tongue?
What interstellar language might we use to converse with
    the dead, blithely trafficking among

asteroids passing at the speed of light? We think
    they call it music, the music of the spheres.
Tonight we wish to share it with those receptive enough
    to care. Do not be moved to easy tears;

we all must learn to grieve the passing moments
    of our days, to take what little solace that we can,
united by the unseen strands securing us together:
    the voices of woman, the voices of man.

Residual Beauty

So slowly does it accrue
that even you begin to notice
after half a century. It manifests

in the clothes you choose,
the jewelry, the flowers
conjured in your yard.

Elusive, hard to startle
(though you often do in dreams),
it settles like a butterfly

on thistle, becomes
for one brief moment
the focus of your attention,

something so utterly
familiar that your looking
makes it new.

VI.

Lyrics Perhaps

A good house is in delicate balance with its surroundings, and they with it. A good house is created of many parts meaningfully assembled. It speaks not just of the materials of which it is made, but of the intangible rhythms, spirits . . .

—E. Fay Jones

The song of Momo Kai: "I went to the town of Gbesseh because someone had died. While there, a storm came and all the people scattered. I lay down and went to sleep. In my sleep a man dressed in pure white came to me. This man told me that he would show me a song and that I should sing it until God told me to stop. The song will have no limits. The man told me that it would be my property. Since I first sang this song, many singers around have made up different parts to it. There is no end. My song goes on forever."

—Lester Monts, from "The Conceptual Nature
of Music Among the Vai of Liberia"

Rock-Skipping on the West Fork

Semis grind to make the grade
    behind us on the hill;
otherwise the summer stream
    is somnolent and still.

Already, son, your arm is strong,
    your aim as straight as mine,
even though I'm thirty-eight
    and you are only nine.

Someday, when you're thirty-eight
    and I am sixty-seven,
I hope that we can come back here
    like truants under heaven

to skip the stones that weighed us down
    in years less kind than these,
and watch them clear the opposite shore
    and vanish into the trees.

Lost Bridge

(for Donald Harington)

Drifting like a lily pad
    upon this manmade lake,
I feel it almost functions as
    an amniotic sac;

and yet, for sunken bluffs, it is
    a river's liquid shroud,
here where I have ventured and
    no swimmer is allowed.

Testing out the boundaries
    between the elements,
I think of those who tried to swallow
    ponds and oceans once;

John Gould Fletcher and Hart Crane,
    a boy I knew in school.
It would only take a sudden
    cramp or fear to pull

me under too. I flirt with death
    then turn to hurry back,
where ropes and buoys help stave off
    encroachment by the lake.

No tourist here would think to trace
    the course of any river,
vanished under waves in what,
    for me, must be forever.

High Wind

The hillside barn tilts precariously
in the wind, flapping a sheet of loose tin.
Inside, its timbers sag and groan like men
who have given up, longing just to see

this through. Earlier, a rainbow in the east.
Whatever that, if anything, portends.
Maybe just the spectrum in our minds.
How light bounces off of that, at least.

Erratic birds churned against the current,
a maneuver requiring all their strength
as an October storm turned up the length
of our estate. The neighbors' horses went

and stood under the only post oak in
their pasture. If I could pray I would pray
for their safety, that the thunderbolt stay
its hand, the lightning take its bright amen

elsewhere. High wind and all the fear
that represents. The tendency to grieve.
To bargain with the power as we perceive
it. Praise the darkest cloud as it draws near.

Famine Village, County Kerry

Roofless, half a dozen stone houses
stand vacant on the austere hillside.
Laid waste by failed crops or the Big Wind
of '39, their occupants escaped or died.

Each year their ghosts return to feast on air,
tables piled high with anything but potatoes,
potato soup, potato pancakes, notable
for their absence. Then heels click to those

reels which make the fiddler's fingers fly,
the poteen flowing freely as their tales
of mirth or woe, the dancers flouncing
dawnward against their incontestable wills.

At daybreak, nothing but these barren hills
set against the MacGillicuddy Reeks,
the dancers all turned back into stone,
the storytellers gone where no one speaks.

From a Busy Interstate

Sparrowhawk on the highline wire,
    fiercest of your kind,
for ransoming the wilderness,
    forgive the likes of mine,

who bid the rivers to turn back,
    the mountains to bow down,
our global sleight-of-hand transforming
    countryside into town.

Next time you flash into tall grass
    to pierce your quarry through,
remember we were hunters once
    as vigilant as you.

The Fox

He crosses the road with his tail
Straight out, moving purposefully.
Our headlights reveal a ghostly
Beard—a baby hare or a quail—

Suspended from the set chin.
It's hard to see why he disturbs
Our sleep within the suburbs,
Or know how he'll survive when

The last pasture is paved over
With parking lots and manicured
Green lawns, the distinction blurred
Between who's prey and predator.

All the wiles of Kingdom Come
Will not preserve you, Brother Fox,
From that rude pestilence which knocks
At both our doorways, waiting, dumb.

Return of the Passenger Pigeons

At first they came by twos and threes,
Congregating in the trees
Like judges. Then it grew dark,
As if the sun had missed its mark
And slipped into oblivion.
All flights were cancelled. Suburban
Lawns were burned up in a twinkling,
A layer of droppings covering
The earth. At night nothing but static.
Lying in bed, we hear the attic
Sag with their increasing weight.
Like us, they seem prepared to wait.

April Foal

(for Soraya and Luciya)

Scrawny yellow pony,
Tallow-tarnished white,
Frisking in the meadow,
Bringing us delight—

If your coat were finer
You would never know,
Born in the wrong season
To have seen it snow,

Born in the wrong pasture
To have heard them tell
About your distant cousin
Upon the carousel,

Who's seen enough of brightness
And color to astound,
But never tasted clover
Nor walked upon the ground.

Simple Gifts

(for Brendan)

They now have toys that play with you,
A thing no proper toy should do,
Reminding me, at age of six,
How my best friends were rocks and sticks.

Higher Education

(An Exhortation to My Students)

May you all receive high marks
    In parenthood and love;
Some things cannot be quantified
    Or graded on a curve.

If you decide to stay single,
    May you discover the pleasure
Of honest work and solitude;
    Success is hard to measure.

And may you take in stride the toughest
    Lesson of them all,
Seeing childhood heroes topple
    From their pedestal.

The only thing that changes is
    Perception and you.
All that glitters isn't gold;
    Sometimes shit glitters too.

Hopefully someday you'll learn
    To tell the difference,
Forgive an old professor who
    Insisted on it once.

Octaves

1. Lost Valley
(for David)

Poets should have named the world;
     no more fusty Latin;
purple petals on the trail
     becoming lords-in-satin.
A bashful weed with yellow blooms
     is suddenly a flower
that you would care to reckon with
     as blondes-in-the-shower.

2. Song of the One-Armed Juggler
(for Sally)

I can no more revise a poem
     written at twenty-one
than I can sever my left arm
     and grow it back again;
and yet I continue trying
     to rearrange the past
as if none of us were dying
     and all of this would last.

Coronal

Silt filters down the mountainside
to form fan-shaped alluvials,
small deltas orphaned
far from any flood-plain.

May-apples near the fence-row
are spinsters under parasols,
waiting for the sun to signal
respite from spring rain.

A heron on the millpond
is minister of stillness,
poised for the next
unwary minnow,

appearing to his victim
like an unexpected avatar,
feet in muck, a sunstruck
thunderhead for diadem.

Forlorn Hope

During the Napoleonic wars,
You were the hapless volunteers
To be first through the fortress wall
Breached by a lucky cannonball,

Your chances of survival nil.
Two centuries later, we still
Long for some vainglorious
Deed that might distinguish us

From the herd, those who would follow
Blindly an ideal that could swallow
Us whole, a metaphoric snare
Whose battle-line is everywhere.

Gaunt brigades of the fallen
Rise up to fight and fall again.
It doesn't help to be clever.
Do you want to live forever?

Exit Poll

Time now to put away the drawn swords
of campaign strategy, the ambitions
thwarted or revealed. Beneath the words
lurk something like our best intentions.
The slogans we repeat may outlive us
like light arriving from a dying star,
no longer part of an organic process
or representative of who we are
or what we think. By the time you hear
what is being said, the meaning will
have altered, the context disappear
like fallen leaves devoid of chlorophyll.
Maybe it all comes down to semantics,
the shamelessness of post-election antics.

Uses of Poetry

Maybe we should emulate
Those poets of Cathay
Who folded poems into boats
And watched them sail away.

GERRY SLOAN is a professor of music at the University of Arkansas in Fayetteville where he recently completed his fourth decade teaching low brass and music history. Born in Oklahoma City in 1947, he was raised in eastern Oklahoma and western Arkansas. His degrees are from Arkansas Tech and Northwestern University. Gerry's poems have appeared in such journals as *Yarrow*, *Negative Capability*, *The Nebraska Review*, *North Dakota Quarterly*, and *The Christian Science Monitor*, plus the *Anthology of Magazine Verse & Yearbook of American Poetry*. An essay won *The Missouri Review* Preternatural Readers Contest in 1987, and he received the 1990 WORDS award in poetry, sponsored by the Arkansas Literary Society. Additionally, he has been a featured reader at the Ozark Poets and Writers Collective. Three chapbooks are *Driving Through Fidelity* (Paper Moon Chapbooks, 1992), *Invisible Guests* (Piccadilly Press, 1993), and *Common Time* (Andy Anders, 1999). This is his first full-length poetry collection. Gerry has five children, four grandchildren, and currently resides in Fayetteville with his wife and daughter. He can be reached, for the foreseeable future, at gsloan@uark.edu.

CPSIA information can be obtained at www.ICGtesting.com
Printed in the USA
LVOW111156290212

270957LV00002B/20/P